SuperCroc FOUND

by **Sally M. Walker**
illustrations by **Philip Hood**

On My Own

SCIENCE

M Millbrook Press/Minneapolis

Text copyright © 2006 by Sally M. Walker
Illustrations copyright © 2006 by Philip Hood

Millbrook Press
A division of Lerner Publishing Group
241 First Avenue North
Minneapolis, MN 55401 U.S.A.

Website address: www.lernerbooks.com

Library of Congress Cataloging-in-Publication Data

Walker, Sally M.
    Supercroc found / by Sally M. Walker ; illustrations by Philip Hood.
        p.   cm. — (On my own science)
    Includes bibliographical references.
    ISBN-13: 978-1–57505–760–6 (lib. bdg. : alk. paper)
    ISBN-10: 1–57505–760–3 (lib. bdg. : alk. paper)
    1. Sarcosuchus imperator—Juvenile literature. 2. Crocodiles, Fossil—Juvenile literature. I. Hood, Philip. II. Title. III. Series.
    QE862.C8W35 2006
    567.9'8—dc22   2004017856

Manufactured in the United States of America
1 2 3 4 5 6 – DP – 11 10 09 08 07 06

To my intrepid explorers Maurice, Alexis, and Susan,
without whom I would not have completed the journey
—P. H.

A Dangerous Dinosaur Eater,
110 Million Years Ago

A thirsty *Ouranosaurus*
stood on the riverbank.
The river seemed quiet and safe.
Down the river, two eyes
poked above the water's surface.
The dinosaur drank.

Suddenly, a giant crocodile
lunged from the water.
The SuperCroc's jaws snapped shut
on the dinosaur's head.
The giant croc dragged the dinosaur
into the water.
The croc's head whipped back and forth.
Its sharp teeth ripped a hunk of meat
from the dying dinosaur.
The hungry crocodile gulped it down.

For many years, SuperCroc ruled the river.

But one day, it died.

Animals ate its flesh.

Its bones lay on the river bottom.

Layers of sand buried them.

After thousands of years,

the bones and the sand turned into stone.

The bones had become fossils.

Would anyone find SuperCroc's fossils?

Desert Discoveries,
Ténéré Desert, Africa, 1965

Slowly, the riverbank changed.

The climate changed too.

The river dried up.

The land became a desert in Africa.

For many years, the wind blew sand
across the land.
The blowing sand scrubbed
the rocky desert floor.
Fossils of trees and animals from long ago
could be seen again.
Some of the fossils belonged to SuperCroc.

In 1965, a French paleontologist
went to the Ténéré Desert in Africa.
His name was Philippe Taquet.
He was looking for fossils.
Fossils taught him about animals
and plants that lived in the past.

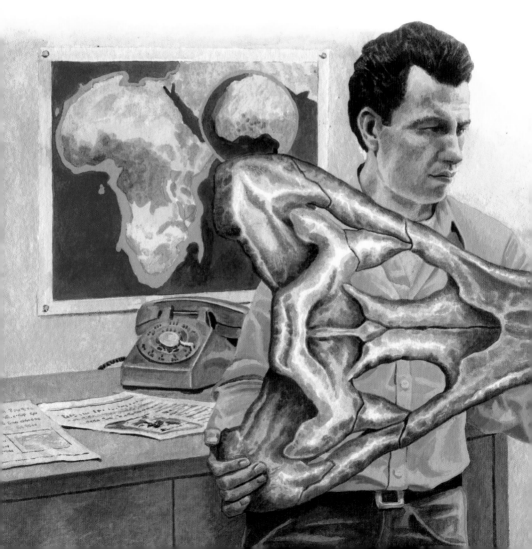

The Ténéré Desert thrilled Taquet.

He found fossils everywhere!

But he didn't see SuperCroc's fossils.

Later, Taquet visited a museum in Niger.

He saw a fossil of a crocodile skull.

It had been found in the Ténéré Desert.

The skull was 3 feet long!

Taquet was surprised at how big it was.

The skull of the largest living croc

was only 2 feet long.

Taquet wanted to study the skull.

He had it sent to France.

Taquet studied the skull
with a woman named France de Broin.
De Broin was another paleontologist.
She had other crocodile fossils.
Her uncle, Albert-Félix de Lapparent,
had found them in Africa in 1947.
De Broin and Taquet compared their fossils.
The two paleontologists
made a surprising discovery.
These bones were not like any other.
No one knew about this kind of crocodile.
It did not exist anymore.
De Broin and Taquet named the crocodile
Sarcosuchus imperator.
Sarcosuchus means "flesh crocodile."
Imperator means "emperor."
They thought their crocodile
was larger than life, like a grand king.

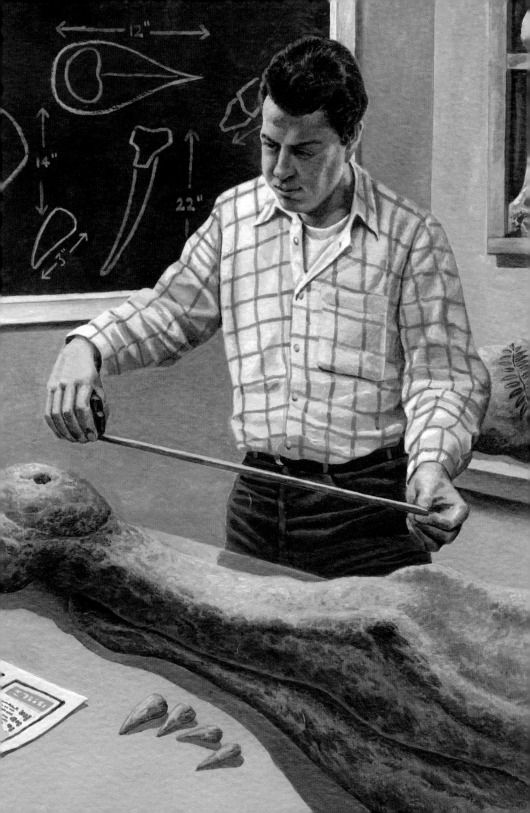

Paleontologists found more
Sarcosuchus bones.

One skull was 5 feet long!

But no one found a complete skeleton.

And no one found SuperCroc's fossils.

Taquet wondered how long *Sarcosuchus* was.

He read about living crocodiles.

He learned that their heads grow larger
as their bodies grow.

Taquet could measure a *Sarcosuchus* skull
and figure out how long its body was.

He measured and decided that *Sarcosuchus*
could have been as long as a bus!

Taquet wished he had a complete skeleton.

Then he would know
exactly what *Sarcosuchus* looked like.

An Amazing Find
Niger, Africa

In 1997, Paul Sereno
traveled to Niger, Africa.
Sereno was a well-known dinosaur hunter.
While looking for fossils, he saw a shape
that looked like a crocodile head.
It was the outline of a crocodile skull.
Sereno knew this kind of skull.
It belonged to a *Sarcosuchus imperator.*
Three years later, he returned to Niger
with a team of workers.
Sereno's team trekked across the hot sand.
They were on a mission.
They planned to dig out
the giant croc's skull.

They measured the skull's outline.

It was 6 feet long!

It was the largest *Sarcosuchus* skull
ever found.

They called it SuperCroc.

Sereno's team brushed sand off the skull.

They marveled at SuperCroc's long snout.

It looked like the snout of a gharial.

The gharial is a modern crocodile.

Its skinny snout helps it catch and eat fish.

But SuperCroc's snout was long enough

to crush a 5-foot-long fish!

Some of Sereno's students

were part of his team.

They searched around SuperCroc's skull.

They found more bones!

Could SuperCroc's whole skeleton be there?

The team could hardly wait to find out.

They dug into the rocky ground.

Carving the rock took days.
The team carefully chipped away
the rock around the skull.
They tunneled under it.
But they left some of the rock
around the skull.
They didn't want to accidentally chip off
any small bits of fossil.
That would ruin it.

Next, the team soaked strips
of burlap cloth in wet plaster.
They wrapped the strips around the skull.
The plaster dried into a hard,
heavy covering.
The covering would protect the skull
from breaking.
Sereno wanted to send the fossil
to his laboratory in Chicago, Illinois.

The next big step
was loading the skull into a truck.
Lifting the skull was tricky.
One slip and the skull
would smash to the ground.
It took nine people to lift
the 800-pound load.
But they did it!
Soon SuperCroc's skull was on its way
to the United States.
During the following weeks,
the team uncovered more
of SuperCroc's bones.

They also found other *Sarcosuchus* bones
near SuperCroc.
Together, all the bones
made half a *Sarcosuchus* skeleton.
The bones were shipped to Sereno's lab.
What would he learn from these fossils?

Questions and Answers
Chicago, Illinois

Sereno's team of paleontologists worked
on SuperCroc's fossils and the other
Sarcosuchus bones for many months.
They carefully drilled away
the plaster and rock.
Sereno grouped the bones.
He found part of the backbone but no tail.
He wanted to know SuperCroc's length.
So he measured SuperCroc's skull.
From that, he figured out
SuperCroc's length.
SuperCroc was almost 40 feet long!
It was longer than any *Sarcosuchus*
ever found!

Next, Sereno wanted to see how
SuperCroc's mouth opened and closed.
But he would never experiment
with a SuperCroc fossil.
It could break.
Instead, he made a rubber mold
of SuperCroc's top and bottom jaws.
From the mold, his team could make
an exact copy of SuperCroc's skull.

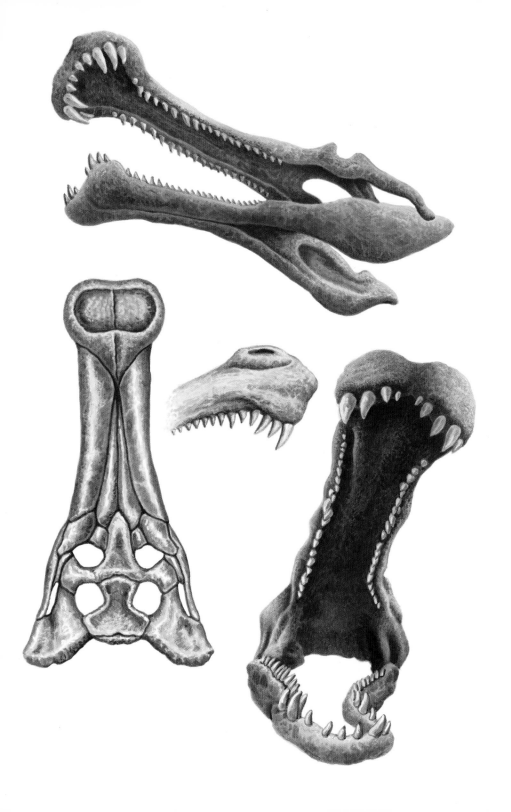

For the first time, Sereno got
a close look at SuperCroc's skull.
SuperCroc's eye sockets
were on top of the skull.
The tip of SuperCroc's snout puzzled him.
He had never seen anything like it.
The tip was large and shaped like a bowl.
The top jaw was a lot longer
than the lower jaw.
The jaws held 132 teeth.
Some were longer than 3 inches.

Sereno wondered if all crocodiles
were like SuperCroc.
He decided to look at modern crocodiles.
They would help him understand how
SuperCroc might have looked and acted.
Sereno studied living crocodiles.
He also talked to crocodile experts,
such as Brady Barr.

Sereno and Barr watched crocodiles
and even helped catch some.
Sereno learned surprising things.
Modern crocs bellow.
But no living croc has a snout
shaped like SuperCroc's.
Sereno thought that SuperCroc's bowl-
shaped snout would have made
a super-loud bellow.

Sereno watched modern crocodiles swim.
Only their eyes and nostrils
poked above the water's surface.
SuperCroc's eyes and nostrils
were in the same place on its head.
Sereno believed that SuperCroc
swam the same way.

Hidden by the water,

a croc swims close to its prey

without being noticed.

Suddenly, the croc lunges from the water.

The croc bites its prey

and drags it into the water.

Sereno thought that SuperCroc

hunted this way too.

And he was sure that SuperCroc

hunted dinosaurs.

The teeth of SuperCroc and living crocs
have the same shape.
But SuperCroc had more teeth.
And SuperCroc's jaws were much more
powerful than a modern croc's jaws.
Animal experts have figured out
that SuperCroc's bite was
18 times more powerful than a shark's bite.
That's strong enough to chomp dinosaurs!

What protected SuperCroc
from a dinosaur's sharp teeth?
Sereno found the answer when he looked
at SuperCroc's bones.
Behind SuperCroc's skull,
Sereno could see two rows of bony plates.
These plates are called osteoderms.
Each osteoderm covered
part of the next one.
They shielded SuperCroc's soft body.

Sereno saw that modern crocs
also have osteoderms.
Their osteoderms cover their backs
and half of their tails like armor.
Perhaps SuperCroc's osteoderms did too.

Sereno learned that crocodiles
bask in the sun to warm their bodies.
But if a croc's body gets too hot, it can die.
Crocs can't sweat to cool off.
Osteoderms keep a crocodile
from overheating.

Osteoderms have many
tubelike blood vessels.
The blood inside them gets hot
when osteoderms heat up in the sun.
The vessels carry hot blood
away from the osteoderms.
The blood flows into cooler parts
of the crocodile's body.
Sereno studied SuperCroc's osteoderms.
It was clear they worked the same way.

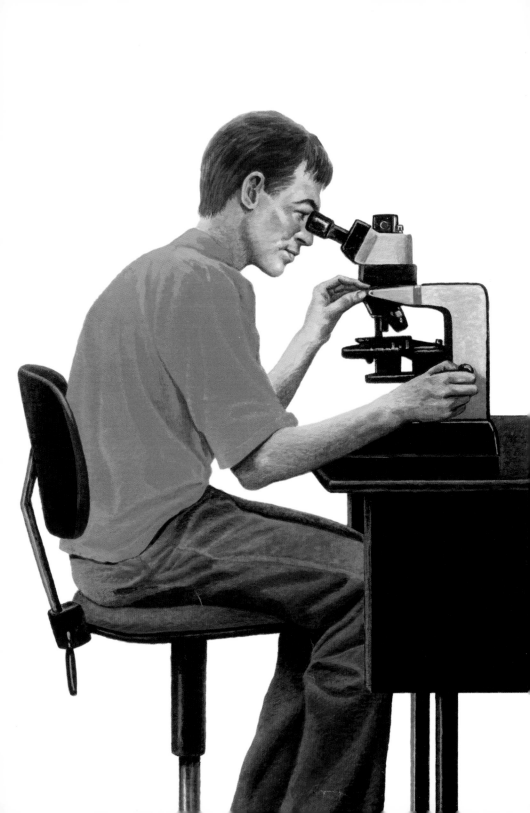

Sereno wondered how old SuperCroc was.

Crocodile experts suggested he look at
SuperCroc's osteoderms.

Each year a croc grows,
an osteoderm gets a new layer of bone.

Sereno's team used a microscope
to look for and count the growth rings.

The rings would also show how
SuperCroc grew.

Sereno knew that dinosaurs grew quickly.

Did SuperCroc grow super fast too?

The growth ring patterns
showed that it didn't.

SuperCroc grew for about 40 years.

Sereno thinks other *Sarcosuchus imperator*
may have lived as long as 100 years.

For Sereno and his team,
SuperCroc's bones were like a giant puzzle.
Some pieces of SuperCroc's puzzle
were missing.
But artists could fill in the empty spaces
with models of the missing bones.
Their fossil copies and fake bones were
used to build a complete skeleton.

To make SuperCroc look alive,
Sereno asked an artist for help.
Gary Staab is well known for his lifelike
models of creatures from long ago.
Sereno told Staab what he had seen
when watching living crocodiles.
On his own, Staab learned more
about crocodiles.
Finally, he had enough information
to make a life-size model of SuperCroc.
The model has skin, scales,
legs, toes, and eyes.
After 110 million years,
we can finally see
how awesome SuperCroc was.

SuperCroc's 6-foot-long skull (*left*) makes the skulls of living crocs seem tiny. The skull of an adult Orinoco crocodile is less than 2 feet long.

SuperCroc was found in the hot, barren Ténéré Desert, near Gadoufaoua, Niger. This area of Africa is very different from the way it looked when SuperCroc was alive. Around 110 million years ago, a large river flowed across a plain. Lush plants and tall trees grew along the riverbanks. Many kinds of animals lived there and were preserved as fossils. The fossil beds near Gadoufaoua are among the richest in the world.

Some fossils found in Brazil appear to be *Sarcosuchus imperator* fossils. If so, they support the theory that 100 million years ago, Africa and South America were connected as one large continent. Perhaps future finds in Brazil will provide more evidence.

Glossary

climate (KLY-muht): the usual weather in a place

fossils (FAH-suhlz): the remains of plants and animals that have turned into stone

osteoderms (AW-stee-oh-durmz): flat, bony plates found on a crocodile's back and tail

paleontologist (PAY-lee-uhn-TAH-luh-jihst): a scientist who studies extinct animals

prey (PRAY): an animal that is hunted and eaten by another animal

***Sarcosuchus imperator* (SAR-koh-soo-kihs ihm-PEER-uh-tuhr):** an extinct kind of crocodile

skeleton (SKEH-luh-tihn): the framework of bones in the body

skull (SKUHL): the bony part of a head

snout (SNOWT): the part of an animal's head that includes its nose, mouth, and jaws

Selected Bibliography

Buffetaut, Eric, and Philippe Taquet. "The Giant Crocodilian *Sarcosuchus* in the Early Cretaceous of Brazil and Niger." *Paleontology* 20 (February 1977): 203–208.

Taquet, Philippe. *Dinosaur Impressions: Postcards from a Paleontologist*. Cambridge: Cambridge University Press, 1998.

Sereno, Paul, Hans Larsson, Christian Sidor, and Boubé Gado. "The Giant Crocodyliform *Sarcosuchus* from the Cretaceous of Africa." *Science* 294 (November 2001): 1516–1519.

Sereno, Paul. "SuperCroc: A Dinosaur's Nightmare." *National Geographic*, December 2001, 84–89.

Further Reading

Sereno, Paul. "SuperCroc: A Dinosaur's Nightmare." *National Geographic*, December 2001, 84–89.

Sloan, Christopher. *SuperCroc and the Origin of Crocodiles*. Washington, DC: National Geographic Society, 2002.

Walker, Sally M. *Crocodiles*. Minneapolis: Carolrhoda Books, Inc., 2004.

Websites

DinoQuest Sahara
http://www.nationalgeographic.com/dinoquest/
Paul Sereno and his team describe their work in Niger, Africa, in 2000. Photographs, notes from the field, and maps provide details on their incredible fossil discoveries, including the SuperCroc find.

SuperCroc—Sarcosuchus imperator
http://www.supercroc.com/
This site is the best resource for everything there is to know about SuperCroc.